F

and the

RESISTANCE TO READING

MIKE LLOYD-JONES

HOWL BOOKS

First published in 2013 by Howl Books,
an imprint of Sounds Together Ltd

The Roots of Resistance

On the 9th November 1806 an English private ship of war anchored off the coast of one of the Tongan Islands. Under orders from the local chief the ship was attacked and most of the crew killed. Among the few allowed to survive was a teenage boy named William Mariner. He was taken under the protection of the tribal chief and for the next four years Mariner lived among the islanders. The boy had been the ship's clerk and so was able to write. When the Tongan chief first saw Mariner's writing he was baffled, because writing was at that time still unknown in the Islands. When Mariner explained to him that through writing, ideas, facts or messages could be recorded and then later read by someone else, the chief's puzzlement turned to fear. Writing was, he acknowledged, a great invention but it would not do at all for the Tongan Islands. If writing were introduced on the Islands, insisted the Tongan chief, *"there would be nothing but disturbances and conspiracies, and he should not be sure of his life, perhaps, another month*".

William Mariner's account of his experiences in the Tongan Islands became a best-selling book when he later returned to England. Readers in the nineteenth century had a great appetite for traveller's tales and the more extraordinary the descriptions of exotic customs, habits and attitudes the better. But to many of those readers the Tongan chief's anxieties about the potential dangers of literacy would have seemed entirely conventional and rational.

Writing in England in 1805, (just about the time that Mariner was sailing towards Tonga) William Playfair, inventor of modern graphical techniques such as the line graph and the pie chart, precisely expressed a common view about education for the masses: "*Industry and a trade are the chief parts of education….reading and writing are not, being but of a very doubtful utility to the labouring class of society.*"

In the nineteenth century, English anxieties about the dangers of mass literacy help to explain why free schooling for all took so long to become established here. When, for example, an attempt was made in 1807 to introduce a bill to establish an elementary school in every parish, the MP Davies Giddy argued in the House of Commons that: "*however specious in theory the project might be, of giving education to the labouring classes of the poor, it would, in effect, be found to be prejudicial to their morals and happiness; it would teach them to despise their lot in life, instead of making them good servants in agriculture, and other laborious employments to which their rank in society had destined them; instead of teaching them subordination, it would render them factious and refractory, as was evident in the manufacturing counties it would enable them to read seditious pamphlets, vicious books, and publications against Christianity; it would render them insolent to their superiors..."*

Charles Adderley, the mid-nineteenth-century vice-president of the government's Committee of the Council on Education, declared that "*any attempt to keep children of the labouring classes under intellectual culture after the very earliest age at which they could earn their living, would be as arbitrary and improper as it would be to keep the boys at Eton and Harrow at spade labour*".

Given this resistance to mass literacy is not surprising that free schooling for all took a long time to establish here. For most of the nineteenth century the most modest steps in England towards universal schooling were hotly resisted. Even tentative moves towards contributing any small sums of public money to support the work of charitable schools were

3

regarded with great suspicion. This resistance was motivated by exactly the same anxieties expressed by the Tongan chief – education for the masses would encourage social unrest, promote worker dissatisfaction and even tend to revolution.

England has never been entirely at ease with the prospect of universal literacy...

The Dismal Record of Standards

Ⅰt was not until 1870 that England adopted a
national system of schools and a further ten
years before school attendance was made
compulsory (and then only up to the age of ten).
Hardly surprising then that contemporary statistics
revealed widespread illiteracy. The 1876 report of the
Registrar General, noted that 16% of men and 22% of
women could not so much as sign their name in the
marriage register.

Even when universal schooling was belatedly
established as a right, expectations of literacy still
remained low. Basic reading, writing and arithmetic
were all that was needed to supply the armies of
clerks now needed to deal with the paperwork
generated in factories and businesses (plus just
enough literacy to provide a growing market for the
increased production of books, papers and magazines
made possible by the application of steam power to
the printing press).

Those expectations remained low throughout the greater part of the twentieth century. But complacency about standards received an initial shock during the Second World War when recruitment surprisingly revealed that many men either could not read at all or had standards of reading so low as to make them functionally illiterate. In the first year of the war nearly a quarter of the 16 and 17 year olds entering the forces were found to be illiterate.

This dawning of concern prompted a number of research projects, some local and small-scale, some more ambitious in scope, that set out to establish the state of reading achievement or, to put it more negatively and using the language of the day, the state of 'reading backwardness'.

The local surveys, in places such as Brighton and Middlesbrough, did not provide reassurance. In Burton-upon-Trent, for example, a survey in 1947 found that "*approximately 23% of children tested had reading ages two years or more below their mental ages*". In Leeds in 1953 a study of 4866 children found that "*19% of them had a reading age two or more years behind their chronological age*". These and other surveys with similar outcomes are a helpful antidote to the often-expressed myth that in primary

6

schools of fifty or sixty years ago 'everyone learned to read'.

Attempts to draw a national picture were no more encouraging. A national survey of 15 year olds carried out in 1948 showed that approximately 30% of them had a reading age more than three years behind their chronological age. Some comfort was drawn from this depressing statistic by drawing the conclusion that this cohort of children had been held back by a disrupted education due to wartime. There was no doubt some truth in this.

Further national surveys – in 1952 and 1956 – provided some encouragement: standards for eleven year olds were found to have risen since 1948 (reflecting probably the greater stability of peacetime schooling) but the findings still contained depressing news. The mean score for the eleven year olds in 1956 was still three months lower than the mean score established in 1938. So although standards had risen post-war they were no better – in fact slightly worse – than they had been pre-war.

Unfortunately it was the immediately post-war standards that became established as the baseline and taking this as the starting point was to result in misleading optimism. In 1966 the Department of Education and Science published a report on *Progress in Reading 1948-1964* which claimed a "*remarkable improvement*" in reading standards. It reached this conclusion on the basis of evidence gathered annually in a reading test given to a representative sample of eleven year olds, each year from 1947 onwards. This showed a substantial improvement over time, but the reality behind this was that the improvement was limited and short-term – in fact what the "*Progress in Reading*" report interpreted as a rise in standards was almost certainly nothing more than a return to the standards of the 1930s following the observed dip in standards during the disruption to schools in wartime.

It is possible to draw a vivid contrast between the complacency of the "*Progress in Reading*" report and the evidence of actual standards. In 1958 the National Child Development Survey began a longitudinal study of 17000 children born during a single week in 1958. The study followed those children into adulthood and revealed, amongst other things, that nearly one in five had low levels of literacy. Those adults had all been in primary school, just beyond the infant years, at the very time when *Progress in Reading* appeared with its complacent judgments about standards.

Whatever lay behind the post-war rise reading standards they quickly stagnated and remained static for forty years. The National Foundation for

Educational Research began to test the reading of a national sample of eleven year olds in 1947 and by the mid-1990s it was possible for an expert analyst to reach the depressing judgment that between 1948 and 1996 "*literacy standards have changed very little*". It is hard to think of any other aspect of national expectation or achievement that had not risen significantly or even dramatically over that same period of time – only standards of reading remained, in the last years of the twentieth century, at the level seen at the end of the 1940s.

The analysis of the year-on-year data gathered by the NFER since 1948 did show a slight improvement in reading score between 1948 and 1952 but revealed that average reading scores then remained more or less unchanged for over a quarter of a century. Then, between 1987 and 1991, a significant decline set in (more or less equivalent to a decline of around six months in reading age) only for that trend to be reversed over the next four years. The position at the end of that interlude of down-and-up was that reading standards were back almost where the series of tests had started in 1948. So reading standards by the mid-1990s were pretty much as they had been just after the Second World War. A later study also found little evidence of improvement through most of the 1990s and concluded in 1997 that "*standards of*

9

reading have remained more or less the same over a long time – since the 1950s". So much for the "*remarkable improvement*" promised in the *Progress in Reading* report.

For the last twenty years or so public accountability for standards has been through the reporting of the assessment outcomes at the end of Key Stage 1 and Key Stage 2. These assessments do not however provide hard evidence about reading accuracy or fluency. For example, at the end of Key Stage 2 the reading tests have traditionally focused on matters such as authorial intent – e.g. *Why has the author included quotations in this text?*

Even taking the KS1 and KS2 outcomes at face value, however, does not provide reassurance. In 2012 thirteen per cent of KS1 children did not even achieve Level 2 in reading. Less than three in four boys and only 81% of girls achieved at least a level 2b. So at the end of Year 2 around a quarter of all children achieved only the level which, as we will see, Ofsted says should be the expectation for all children at the end of Year 1.

Current KS2 results do not provide an assured sense of uplift. In 2012 13% of children did not achieve a Level 4 and there are widespread concerns that even a Level Four is no guarantee of a good standard and considerable evidence that this level actually masks for many pupils a considerable degree of low achievement. Sir Michael Wilshaw, Her Majesty's Chief Inspector of Schools, has said, "*We should raise the bar because a lot of children who are achieving the national average, particularly the lower end of level four, are not achieving the five A* to C grades five years after they leave primary school.*" A follow-up study in 2012 found that almost a third of pupils who reached level four at 11 failed to gain a good GCSE in English at the age of 16.

Dismal and depressing as is this long record of dismal standards, it does have two significant lessons from which we can learn. The first is that the notion of a past golden age in which reading was effectively taught to all, leading to something like universal literacy, is a myth. The second lesson is that the methods of teaching reading in the past have not proved notably successful. And this might seem to be an argument against phonics – because another widely-held belief is that phonics is the traditional way in which reading used to be taught. But, as we shall see, this is another myth.

The myth of 'traditional' phonics

One of the persistently obstructive myths about phonics is that it is a return to 'traditional methods'. It is, for a start, particularly unhelpful to depict the contemporary focus on phonics as a return to traditional approaches – because, as the analysis of past standards in the previous chapter clearly shows, reading has never been well taught in this country and that whatever methods were acceptable at any time gone by, would certainly not be judged to be good enough for today. But, because the myth about 'traditional phonics' is so persistent, so ingrained, it is worth clarifying the historical record.

In one version of the myth, phonics was *the* method until about forty years ago – for example a piece in the *Daily Mail* on 21 January 2011 described phonics as a "*method of teaching reading which was ditched in the seventies*". If we go back to the sixties, however, and look at what was being said about the teaching of reading then, it certainly does not provide evidence for any idea of 'traditional phonics'.

The *Plowden Report*, the outcome of a massive inquiry into the whole of primary education and published in 1966, did not reach the topic of reading until page 212 where it asserted that so far as the systematic teaching of reading was concerned: *"...the most successful infant teachers have refused to follow the wind of fashion and to commit themselves to any one method...Children are helped to read by memorising the look of words and phrases, often with the help of pictures, by guessing from a context which is likely to bring them success and by phonics, beginning with initial sounds. They are encouraged to try all the methods available to them and not to depend on only one method."*

The Plowden Committee was ill-equipped to make useful recommendations on the teaching of reading. Lady Plowden and her colleagues were, to begin with, working under the handicap that they took at face value the official line that reading standards were going up. But the Committee laboured under the additional disadvantage that they were, in any case, far more interested in the development of the wider curriculum than in reading, writing and mathematics – for example, the report devoted 66 paragraphs to religious education, nearly twice as many as it gave to reading, writing, speaking and drama combined.

What is striking, however, is the picture the *Plowden Report* provides about the teaching of reading: it describes what is clearly a mixture of methods, with phonics (and only partial phonics at that) coming last in the list. There is no suggestion that phonics is the dominant method – or even any suggestion that there is a choice to be made between methods. On the contrary, what the Report notes with evident approval is a mixture of approaches in the hands of teachers who do not "*commit themselves to any one method*".

The description of mixed methods painted by the Plowden Report gives us a picture of expectations around 50 years ago. But anyone who thinks that the rot set in with Plowden and that phonics was the traditional approach before the swinging sixties, let them look at the picture drawn by the distinguished reading researcher Joyce Morris who in a 1954 investigation made a thorough study of reading in a sample of sixty primary schools. She found that all sixty of the schools used mixed methods and that the range of approaches within the mix included the alphabetic method, the phonic method, look-and-say and the sentence method. In her report Joyce Morris, writing in the late 1950s, commented that a "*mixed method is now most frequently advocated and used*".

So the mixture of methods was clearly established by the 1950s, long before Plowden. In yet another version of the 'traditional' phonics myth it was *the* method before the Second World War. Once again the facts do not support this belief. In 1933, for example, an official report from the Board of Education (as it was then called) declared:

"*Much attention has been paid in this country to methods of teaching reading to a group of children, and a variety of methods is employed by different teachers. In all the first step is to secure word recognition; in the old 'look and say' method the child learns to recognise words by their appearance through their repeated occurrence in simple reading matter, while the various 'phonic' methods aim at making the child independent of his teacher by giving him a method by which he can discover the pronunciation of a word for himself and analyse longer words into their phonetic elements. In the more recent 'sentence' method the child is introduced to words in the performance of their natural function as components of a complete sentence, and thus learns to recognise them as a whole. Each of these methods emphasises important elements in learning to read, and most teachers borrow something from each of them...*"

15

Here we have, thirty years before the Plowden Report, the same mixture of methods. And note too that 'look and say' (often regarded as another modern perversion) was being described in 1933 as an 'old' method. It was 'old' indeed – a report written by one of Her Majesty's Inspectors of Schools in 1877 refers to the "*very general adoption of a look-and-say method of teaching*".

So going back nearly a hundred years the record shows not the universal use of phonics but a mixture of methods, in which some form of phonics may have played a part. If there was a time when phonics was something like the standard and principal method of reading teaching it lies for the most part beyond living memory, in the earliest years of the twentieth century (for example the intriguing *Dale Method*, developed by Miss Nellie Dale in 1899) and the second half of the nineteenth century (for example '*Reading Without Tears*' published in 1857).

So the fact of the matter is that the traditional or standard approach to the teaching of reading for the best part of a hundred years or more has not been phonics but a mixture of methods – a mixture that will be analysed later in this book.

The point of this historical digression is not in any way to ascribe any positive value to these mixed methods. Indeed the depressing picture of standards

16

over time would not encourage anyone to reintroduce an approach that had been traditional. The fact is that phonics teaching as advocated now, is nothing like any traditional method – it is far more effective than any traditional method and what is now resisted by the opponents of phonics is not a return to something from the educational museum, but a move forward to something more effective than anything widely used in the past.

- 4 -

"Phonicsphobia"

In 1953 J C Daniels and Hunter Diack, two researchers at the University of Nottingham Institute of Education, wrote a pair of articles for the *Head Teachers' Review*. They argued in these pieces that the established approach of mixed methods in the teaching of reading was inconsistent and ineffective. In its place they outlined their ideas for a fresh approach which they described as 'the phonic word method'.

In a subsequent pamphlet, *Learning to Read*, Daniels and Diack stressed the importance of replacing the current obsession with whole-words with a focus on the letters in those words. *"An alphabet,"* they wrote, *"is a system of symbols for sounds and these symbols are written down in the order in which the sounds are made. A printed word is a time-chart of sound. The act of reading is the act of*

18

translating those time-charts into the appropriate sounds, the sounds being associated with things, events or emotions."

These two researchers no doubt expected that their ideas and arguments would be subjected to critical debate and even counter-argument. What they were not prepared for was the outrage and fury that was released against them from teachers and others intensely angered by Daniels' and Diack's insistence that the starting point in reading was the letters in words. The abuse was not only verbal – according to one account Dr Daniels was actually physically assaulted after one lecture in which he criticised the traditional hotchpotch of mixed methods.

What Daniels and Diack had uncovered was that advocacy of phonics triggers in some an irrational, visceral response – opponents of phonics often react against the method with an impassioned hostility. It was left to another distinguished reading researcher, Joyce Morris, to analyse this phenomenon and to give it a name – *'Phonicsphobia'*.

In a lecture Joyce Morris has described her own experience of the anger that can be generated against anyone who advocates teaching phonics. In 1953 she published, in the journal *Educational Research*, an article entitled *'Teaching children to read: The relative effectiveness of different methods of teaching reading. The place and value of phonics'*. A little time afterwards she encountered in a restaurant a former teaching colleague who announced that she was "*very angry*" about the *Educational Research* article. Joyce Morris recalled in her lecture how this teacher then "*launched into a diatribe about phonics which was so irrational and emotionally-charged that I realised that my old colleague had become 'phonicsphobic', apparently incapable of distinguishing between fact and opinion about a subject, the mere mention of which disturbed her equilibrium."*

Joyce Morris coined the term *'phonicsphobia'* for this kind of irrational reaction against phonics because of its familial resemblance to other phobias that provoke reactions that can include fear, hatred and prejudice. "*Phonicsphobics*", Joyce Morris has said, "*are people suffering from a pathological condition which, if they are in a position of influence, can and does have serious implications for literacy learners, student and practising teachers and the provision of published resources to aid them in their respective tasks."*

It's over twenty years since Dr Joyce Morris created the 'phonicsphobia' label to characterise the irrational, emotional recoil from the idea of teaching phonics. In the time that has passed, despite all the attempts to improve the understanding of phonics (not to mention despite all the money that has been spent), the condition of 'phonicsphobia' seems, if anything, more infectious than ever. It's certainly more evident. Any survey of anti-phonics argument will take you on a gloomy inspection tour of 'phonicsphobia' suffering - a sort of virtual outpatients department where every symptom of 'phonicsphobia', every tic and spasm, is explicitly on view.

The symptoms that identify phonicsphobia include more than just the hysterical anger aroused in its sufferers whenever phonics is positively mentioned. The phonicsphobics are also compelled to deceive – through invention or misrepresentation of the case for phonics – and to spread anxiety by insisting that the teaching of systematic, synthetic phonics will have dire consequences.

Are all those who declare themselves to be against phonics actually *phonicsphobic*? Almost certainly not. Many have been innocently misled by anti-phonics propaganda and repeat what they have heard because they think it must be true. But the stubborn persistence with which the voices of anti-phonic protest repeat arguments that are demonstrably wrong (and in some cases arguments that do not make any sense) indicates that opposition to phonics has a psychological or sociological causation that runs much deeper than just a belief in an alternative method of teaching reading.

But in order to anatomise anti-phonics arguments and lay bare its inventions, misunderstandings and paralogisms, we need to set out clearly what is being opposed. We need to see what phonics is all about and why teaching systematic, synthetic phonics is to be a statutory requirement in the National Curriculum from 2014.

Systematic Synthetic Phonics

The starting point for systematic, synthetic phonics is the alphabetic code. Letters in words are used to represent the sound that we hear when that word is spoken. Note that the letters do not 'make' sounds (the alphabet is, after all, silent) the letters 'represent' sounds. The alphabet is used as a code to represent the sounds within words and systematic, synthetic phonics sets out to teach children how to unlock that code. By teaching children to decode – by blending the sounds represented in that word, all the way through from left to right – children can be prepared to tackle reading confidently and successfully.

Two technical terms are helpful at this point – 'phoneme' and 'grapheme'. A phoneme is an individual speech sound within a spoken word – the word 'shop' for example consists of three phonemes - /sh/o/p/. A grapheme is a letter (or letters) that represents one of the phonemes in a word. For example, there are three graphemes in the word 'rain' (r-ai-n).

All modern Western European languages work in the same way. They are alphabetic. A code in which a sequence of speech sounds is represented by a sequence of letters. Some languages use a very simple code. In those languages there is more-or-less a one-to-one correspondence between the graphemes and the phonemes. Any one phoneme is generally spelled in the same way and any particular grapheme usually represents only one particular phoneme. Spanish, for example, has a comparatively simple code. In most cases a Spanish speaker can tell from the sound of a word how it must be spelled and, conversely, can usually derive the pronunciation of a word from its spelling.

English by contrast has a complex code. At the heart of the complexity lies the problem that there are just twenty six letters in our alphabet and yet our language uses around 44 speech sounds. Because of this restriction – and also because of the way in which our language has changed over time – there are two particular aspects to this complexity.

Firstly the same phoneme can be represented by more than one grapheme. For example, the sound at the beginning of the words 'cat' and 'kitchen' is the same – yet in one word the phoneme is represented by a 'c' and in the other word by a 'k'.

Secondly the same grapheme can represent more than one phoneme. For example the grapheme in the middle of the word 'cat' represents a different sound to the same grapheme in the middle of the word 'was'.

The relationship between a grapheme and a phoneme is described as a grapheme-phoneme correspondence (GPC) and the backbone of systematic, synthetic phonics teaching is a structured sequence of each GPC to be taught. The sequence sets out not only all the grapheme-phoneme correspondences that need to be taught but also the order in which to teach them.

The order is important because a good systematic, synthetic phonics programme will start by teaching what is sometimes called the 'simple code'. At this stage the aim is to give children a simplified but working knowledge of how our alphabetic system works – enough to be able to read many hundreds of words – and which will enable them by the end of the first year in school (the reception year) to have been able to read hundreds of books.

This teaching of the simple code typically begins with a set of around six or seven graphemes – a common starter set is *s, a, t, p, i, n*, though others are possible. Within a week or two children have learned enough to be able to read a good number of simple words. As the weeks go by children are taught more and more of these GPCs. *Letters and Sounds*, the phonics scheme that is believed to be the one most commonly used in England, lists around 50 of these GPCs to be taught to children in the reception class.

In the second year in school (paradoxically called in England 'Year 1') children build on their basic knowledge of how the alphabetic system works by being introduced to the complex code. Through this stage children learn about the way in which the same phoneme may be represented by different graphemes – and the way in which the same grapheme may represent more than one phoneme. A key focus during Year 1 will be the so-called 'long' vowels. Our language teems with words that contain these long vowels and it is probably here that the greatest complexity in the alphabetic code is to be found.

From the beginning of their phonics teaching children also learn two key skills – blending and segmenting. Blending is the skill of putting the sounds represented in a word together to 'build' that word. Segmenting is the reverse skill – starting with a word and breaking it down into its constituent phonemes. Blending is needed for reading and segmenting is needed for spelling.

26

The way in which a good phonics programme provides a comprehensive and systematic 'route-map' for teaching the grapheme-phoneme correspondences is key to effective systematic, synthetic phonics. The order in which those GPCs are to be taught is also important. A high-quality phonics programme introduces the GPCs in a way which steadily builds on learning and introduces new challenges (e.g. two-letter graphemes) in a gradual and logical way.

The aim is to build up an understanding of the concept of the alphabetic code, a growing knowledge of grapheme-phoneme correspondences and the skills both to blend those GPCs to read words and to segment known words into their phonemes so that an attempt can be made to write them.

So at the heart of systematic, synthetic phonics is the unlocking of the alphabetic code. The French word for illiteracy is, very sensibly, '*analphabétisme*' which neatly captures the way in which reading depends on a good understanding of the way in which the letters in words provide the key insight into what those words are. But, as we shall see, those who are opposed to phonics are, or pretend to be, blind to the crucial information held by the letters in words.

Word Blindness

The anti-phonics movement is even prepared to pick an argument with the alphabet. Decoding is ultimately unworkable, they assert, because English is "not a phonetic language". They set out to depict the letters in words as mysterious, arbitrary and impenetrable.

However, a curious feature of this line of argument is that those wielding it often reveal, inadvertently, that in fact they know very well that the spelling of every word represents its sound and often show, in the course of their quarrel with the alphabet, that they have a very close knowledge of the relationships between letters and the phonemes they can represent.

You see this in the deployment of one very basic weapon that is repeatedly used against phonics. The trick used is invented spelling – for example "*Fonics iz Krazie*". The intention is apparently to discredit phonics by suggesting that it doesn't apply in the real world because spelling is not consistent. But the argument immediately backfires. It concedes the very point it is trying to attack. Those who wield this weapon show that they know perfectly well that letters in words are used to represent the sounds we hear in those words and *'fonics is krazie'* can be understood because we know how to apply our knowledge of sound-spelling correspondences to read even words that we have not seen before.

Those who deploy the *"phonics doesn't work because our language is not phonetic"* argument depend in part on concealing the fact that systematic, synthetic phonics sets out to teach both the simple and the complex code. These critics delight in producing lists of words that they claim can't be decoded, when in fact they are easily decodable once children have been taught the complex code.

Once again, their argument backfires because in alleging that their lists of words cannot be decoded they draw attention to the very features of the complex code that systematic, synthetic phonics sets out to teach. For example, they point out that the same letter can represent more than one phoneme – for example the letter 'o ' in the words 'so' and 'not'. In producing examples like this these critics display their own knowledge of the complex code, but pretend that this knowledge is to be hidden from children.

A common approach is to use a cluster of words with similar spelling but which are pronounced differently – *cough, though, tough,* and *through* are frequent examples – to argue that spelling is capricious and idiosyncratic. This is then used to argue that the case for phonics cannot be made – that phonics is an unreliable guide and that it is irrational to expect children to be able to decode. But the reality is that spelling to sound-correspondences are not random and uniquely quirky – words like *cough, though, tough* and *through* are all easily decodable, once children have been taught the complex code.

Another of the tricks used by the anti-phonics movement is to conceal the significant difference between phonics for reading and the place of phonics in the learning of spelling. This difference is very important because the application of phonics in reading is not exactly equivalent to the challenge of knowing how to spell an unknown word. For example, if you do not know how to spell the word 'physics' you will probably guess that it will begin with either an 'f' or a 'ph'. But you will need a dictionary (or to make an informed guess) to know which is right. But in reading, both 'f' and 'ph' reliably represent the sound that we hear at the beginning of words like *'fish'* and *'physical'*. In other words turning the spelling of a word into its 'sound' is much less difficult than turning the sound of a word into its correct spelling. Which is why phonics can be thoroughly taught before children are seven, while the securing of accurate spelling takes much longer and requires additional teaching that builds on phonics but includes a lot more.

As Marilyn Jager Adams, a great expert on learning to read, has written: "*there is considerably more entropy in sound-to-spelling than in spelling-to-sound*". In other words spelling is more ambiguous than reading - decoding accurately is a much easier process than spelling correctly. So when propagandists attempt to make the alphabet seem chaotic by producing lists of homophones – such as '*knows*' and '*nose*', '*pair*' and '*pear*' and so on – they are being devious. All of these words are regularly and easily decodable by children who have been taught the complex code. The development of fully accurate spelling is a separate issue - it builds on phonics but is separate from it.

So it comes to this. One form of attack on phonics maintains that there is no deep order to sound-spelling correspondences - in the process of arguing this the critics use examples that show they have a very good understanding of that deep order. A

31

variant of this form of attack is to maintain that the order is so complex that no one could ever learn it.

In the face of this obfuscation, systematic, synthetic phonics has a rational response. It does not pretend that sound-spelling correspondences are a simple matter in English – as they are, relatively speaking, in Finnish or Serbo-Croat. But it does set out to codify the complexity – to make clear the structure of the way in which the sounds of words are represented in English – and it does teach, in a logical and structured sequence, the range of sound-spelling correspondences, from the simple to the complex, that will give children easy and confident access to independent reading.

As an alternative, the critics of phonics offer not a rational process but a piece of wishful thinking – children, they believe, can learn to read by guesswork...

7

Keep the children guessing

What do those opposed to systematic, synthetic phonics advocate as the right strategy for children learning to read? Hard as it may be to believe, the method they support is basically that children should *guess* the words in a book.

They take their lead from an American movement (it could not be even loosely described as a 'school of thought') which is usually referred to as the 'whole language' approach. This method is based on the view that the act of reading is a *'psycholinguistic guessing game'* in which phonics, if it plays a part at all, is merely one of a number of 'cues' that enable the child to 'predict' the words on the page.

As we will see this theory is completely unsupported by any evidence but it is worth examining how such nonsense ever came to be proposed let alone taken seriously. The theory emerged from a study of the mistakes readers make when reading aloud. An analysis of common errors that these readers make was alleged to show that they use a range of 'cues' – including guessing a word from its context – and from this analysis it was concluded that the integration of strategies was the basis of efficient reading. It was then but a short step to asserting that these are the strategies that children should learn to orchestrate in order to become efficient readers. According to this view, reading was a process of 'sampling text in order to construct meaning' and phonics had either only a minor part to play or – in some versions of the theory – no place at all.

It is hard to understand why this nonsense was ever thought to pass muster on its first outing. But, surprisingly, it was quite widely accepted – partly because it clearly represented no challenge to the prevailing orthodoxy in American classrooms where 'mixed methods' of teaching reading were as ubiquitous as in England.

Keith Stanovitch, perhaps the most highly regarded reading researcher in the world, has described what happened when he and another researcher set out to confirm one of the main planks of the 'whole language' theory – that the use of context to recognise words is a major factor in fluent reading. To Stanovitch's admitted "surprise" his research showed that context was not used by good readers – it was poor readers who relied on context to help them pick their way through a text. In other words, the 'psycholinguistic guessing game' turned out to have stood the reading process on its head. Good readers didn't need to guess because they could *decode* – guessing, far from being the natural process of reading, was all that children had to fall back on when they didn't have efficient decoding skills.

And gradually, bit by bit, the case for teaching word guessing proved to be based on a whole series of such misunderstandings or misrepresentations. For example, another of its planks was that readers did not pay significant attention to the letters in words. When scientific experiments were set up to examine this idea it turned out to be completely false.

Another myth promoted by those who advocated word-guessing was that readers proceed not by attending to words or letters but by predicting what word or words would be likely to 'come next'. But when this idea was tested, experimental research showed that less than one in a hundred readers could successfully predict the average next noun, verb or adjective.

So gradually the central thrust of the 'whole language' movement - that children could guess or predict their way through a text without needing to decode the words – was shown to be completely baseless and unworkable. Nevertheless the central idea retained its hold on the mind of many American teachers.

In England many teachers had never heard of the 'psycholinguistic guessing game' but its central idea – that systematic teaching of phonics was unimportant and unnecessary – had become an institutionalised part of teacher education and the training of primary teachers typically ignored the scientific evidence about learning to read and promoted instead an entirely mythical view of the reading process as being dependent on the sampling of a range of cues in which phonics might at best play a minor or incidental part..

So to this day in England 'word-guessing' remains stubbornly rooted in the everyday folk psychology of how to teach reading and is firmly established in the classroom approaches of probably most teachers. When children hesitate or seem 'stuck' over a word, these teachers instinctively prompt the child to guess the word from context, picture or some other clue.

In May 2013 the National Foundation for Educational Research produced a report based on a survey of nearly one thousand primary schools. The evidence gathered showed that 67% of the teachers in the survey believed that children should use a "variety of different methods" to recognise words. The methods identified included context cues and picture cues. In other words, guessing.

The consequence of this perpetuation of 'mixed methods' (guessing from context, pictures, initial sounds and other cues) is that reading development is for so many children slow, partial and ineffective. Because these methods have traditionally produced only patchy outcomes teachers do not expect to see significant progress or widespread success, so they regard the standards achieved as normal and rate themselves as successful teachers of reading. As we will see these teachers mistakenly judge as 'good readers' children who can only guess at unfamiliar words and are unable to read accurately even simple words.

Of course some children transcend the limitations of this mis-teaching and learn to read successfully and enthusiastically. They are able to piece together the alphabetic code for themselves. These children have almost invariably been well-supported at home, through growing up in environments where books and print generally had a high profile and a high status. These children have been read to, have had books of their own, and have grown up nurtured by an encouragement born of a complete confidence that they will be successful

37

readers. In the absence of proper teaching of the code, these children are able to use their experience of books and reading to infer the code for themselves – in effect the self-teaching of phonics.

But children who do not grow up in such virtuous and well-endowed circumstances are abandoned to struggle. The children who are most disadvantaged by the avoidance of systematic, synthetic phonics are those who have, traditionally, always been left on the margins of literacy. These children make up the bulk of the twenty-five to thirty per cent of those who, for as long as we can remember, have, as a result of being expected to guess from pictures, context or other clues, been left with reading and writing skills so limited that they amount to being functionally illiterate.

If you wanted to ensure that this 'underclass' of children continued to be excluded from the advantages of literacy then you could not find a better, more efficient way of perpetuating this social exclusion than by resisting the teaching of systematic, synthetic phonics.

8

Odds, Ends and Wholes

Children taught through the standard muddle of 'mixed methods' (a euphemistic term for what is actually a rag bag of odds and ends) have to treat each word on the page as a special case. They are expected to draw on a range of so-called strategies and, word by word, somehow decide which strategy provides the right answer. This process of guessing – sometimes dressed up as problem-solving or 'working out' the word – can only work when the text has been deliberately designed to make guessing possible.

In some early reading books, for example, pictures are deliberately designed to bypass any word recognition process whatsoever. Using those books children can appear to read what is on the page without even looking at the print at all. Placing a picture of a ball above the word 'ball' means that children can mimic the process of reading effortlessly and without having learned anything about the process of reading. As the books progress in

39

supposed difficulty, this simplest type of picture cue can be replaced by a more sophisticated version where a more elaborate illustration is used to 'cue' an entire sentence or sentences. This might not matter if it were not that some teachers appear not to know the difference between picture-recognition and reading. According to the NFER's survey of 14 case-study schools in 2012, teachers specifically mentioned that they encouraged the use of picture cues in their teaching of reading.

Another way of making guesswork easy is to use highly predictable language. One form of this is to use repetition – where the same word and often the same phrase is used over and over again. Now patterned and predictable phrasing is of course a natural and valuable part of traditional stories and rhymes. But some reading schemes exploit repetition as a device to circumvent the development of word recognition. Words and phrases are repeated not for literary effect but in order to enable children to use their memory to create the illusion of reading. Children working with these texts are gaining no real insight into the fundamental nature of reading and no opportunity to see the utility of phonic decoding. The greatest problem is that teachers, lacking proper understanding of the process, will mistake recall of a pattern of words for the process of reading. As we shall see when we come to examine the Y1 Phonics Screening Check, teachers commonly mistake this kind of behaviour for genuine independent reading.

A more explicit reliance on memorisation is seen when teachers expect children to learn words as 'wholes', by sight. In this technique children are expect to commit the appearance of the word to visual memory. The limits of this technique should be all too obvious, but visual memory was identified as a standard teaching strategy in the NFER survey mentioned earlier.

The idea that children should learn words as a visual configuration goes back at least as far as the beginning of the nineteenth century and the attempt to teach children using this method is still common in classrooms in England. Typically the children will be shown a target word on a flashcard (these days sometimes on the interactive whiteboard) and the children will be asked to remember the look of the word. The features of the word that children are expected to attend to in their attempt at memorising depend on the word itself. In one word it may be length. Another word may be described as having some kind of picture within it - e.g. the two 'eyes' in the word 'moon'. In another word it may be the distribution of ascenders and descenders. And so on.

It might be thought self-evident that the proper and obvious salient feature of any word is its spelling, but a focus on individual graphemes is at odds with the whole word approach and in using it teachers draw attention to any and every typographical feature of a word except the one thing reliable – its sequence of letters. It comes as no surprise that one notable experiment showed that when children appeared to be learning to recognise whole words from flashcards they were actually remembering the word by some incidental detail on the flashcard – for example a smudge or thumbprint on the card.

Recognising whole words by memorising the appearance of the word (sometimes known as the 'look-and-say' approach) is highly problematic. The capacity to remember words as whole-patterns is highly limited and in any case highly inefficient. As Professor Martin Kozloff points out, a child who makes the effort to learn ten words in this way is left recognising on sight just the ten words. But a child who learns ten grapheme-phoneme correspondences is able to read hundreds of words, including of course words that the child has never met in print before – let alone had to commit to visual memory.

A surprisingly widespread myth is that phonics programmes do teach many words by sight – for example, the *Letters and Sounds* phonics programme is often accused by the critics of phonics of advocating the sight-teaching of what are called in that programme 'tricky words'. According to the myth these words cannot be decoded – they are sometimes wrongly described as '*words for which phonics doesn't work*'. In fact the *Letters and Sounds* guidance says quite explicitly (page 64) that 'tricky' words are ones that have "*unusual or untaught GPCs*". In other words they are entirely phonically decodable when children have been taught the phonic knowledge required. These 'tricky words' are ones that are so common that children need to read them early on and *Letters and Sounds* shows teachers how to introduce the phonic knowledge that enables children to decode these words.

There are perhaps less than ten words that children may reasonably be expected to learn as 'wholes' – these are words like *one* and *the*. These very few and very common words use the alphabetic code in such an idiosyncratic way that it is not necessary for children to attempt to sound them out. Applying 'sight-learning' to any more than this tiny handful of words is a pointless waste of time.

The fact of the matter is that all the approaches that make up the 'mixed methods' of reading are inefficient and – worse still – actually mask the lack of progress in reading because teachers confuse

43

guessing with accurate reading. Worst of all these methods actually act as a distraction from the key insight into the relationship between letters and the sounds we hear in words.

Teachers under the spell of 'mixed methods' are actively misleading children about the nature of the reading process and diverting teaching away from the critical path of developing the phonic knowledge and skills that enable children to become accurate at decoding the words on the page.

Given a reliance on this muddled hotchpotch of odds and ends - the mixed methods combining unsystematic, ineffectual and inefficient approaches - it is no wonder so many children find reading so difficult. What is more remarkable is that some people clearly have an interest in keeping things that way.

9

Climate Change: The Rose Review and After

In June 2005 the Department for Education and Skills asked Jim Rose, a former Chief Inspector of Primary Education at Ofsted, to carry out a review of the teaching of early reading. The trigger for this had been a report of the Select Committee on Education which had been following up persistent criticism of the phonics content within the then-current National Literacy Strategy.

When in March 2006 Jim Rose produced his final report ('Independent Review of the Teaching of Early Reading') it concluded that "*The knowledge, skills and understanding that constitute high quality phonic work should be taught as the prime approach in learning to decode (to read) and to encode (to write/spell) print.*"

The recommendations of the Rose Review were immediately accepted by the Secretary of State and systematic, synthetic phonics became national policy. The reaction against this was predictably fierce. It was denounced as '*narrow*' and '*reductionist*' and treating teachers as though they were technicians.

The General Secretary of the National Union of Teachers objected to the *"promotion of a single fashionable technique"* and at the NUT's annual conference, held shortly after the publication of the Rose Review, a member of the union's executive was reported as saying *"phonics is s-t-uh-p-i-d"*.

An additional obstacle was that the clarity of the government's central message on phonics was obscured because at the same time schools were receiving contrary messages from some government agencies. The Labour Government had allowed an extraordinary position to develop in which a range of publicly funded bodies seemed able to pursue individual policies orthogonal to national policy. In some educational quangos - for example the chronically dysfunctional *Qualifications and Curriculum Authority* – individual officials behaved at times as though they believed that they were entitled to issue whatever guidance they pleased.

One example vividly illustrates the stones that were thrown up in the path of the implementation of the Rose Review. The DfES decided that the KS1 national curriculum for English should be amended to reflect directly the implications of Rose. The QCA, the body responsible for the National Curriculum (and notoriously attached to the mixed methods of word guessing), drafted a limp amendment and put it out for public consultation. The Secretary of State, acting under advice, rejected QCA's proposal as inadequate and the Department prepared a tougher version that was laid before Parliament and became law. So the QCA's advice had been rebuffed. However, the QCA was also responsible for maintaining the electronic on-line version of the National Curriculum and what they actually proceeded to put up on their National Curriculum website was not the version that had been agreed by Parliament but their own original, lukewarm proposal.

A blurring of focus nationally was replicated at local level too – because many local authority advisers and school improvement partners were actively opposed to phonics and colluded with poor teaching and low standards. After the Rose Review every local authority was funded to employ a consultant to promote phonics in all schools but the quality of these consultants was variable (some had little or no relevant experience) and even the best consultants were often able to make little headway without the backing of more senior colleagues in the local authority. The National Strategies (NS), a government agency, was tasked with, amongst other things, the responsibility of monitoring the implementation of phonics across each local authority, but in practice a lack of alignment around

47

phonics across different NS policy teams and, in particular, weaknesses in the way in which the NS held LAs to account at the highest level meant that local authorities were able if they wished to ignore phonics or even actively undermine it.

On the back of the Review the government published an outline phonics programme (called *Letters and Sounds*) which was distributed free. Many schools took it up but used it only in a partial and limited way – most commonly short-changing children by teaching only the first part, the simple code. To make matters worse schools routinely put themselves in the fatally contradictory position of trying to teach *Letters and Sounds* in combination with the mixed methods of word guessing.

The Rose Review was an excellent piece of work that effectively cleared the ground and marked out an unambiguous line on the best practice in teaching early reading. It deftly avoided getting bogged down in sterile disputes and set out clear guidance on what primary schools should do to teach reading well. As a backdrop to a national focus on phonics it was straightforward and to the point. But as a spur to action it lacked a critical element which the government of the day was unable – or more accurately, unwilling - to provide. Teeth.

As a consequence, although a little phonics was now more commonly thrown into the mix, the haphazard muddle of word guessing from clues, remained (as it does to this day) the established approach to reading in the majority of primary schools. More than five years after his report Jim Rose had to acknowledge that "*we have not yet reached the tipping point where high-quality teaching of phonics is the norm*".

When in 2010 the Labour Government was replaced by the Coalition Government, Nick Gibb the new Minister for Schools arrived at the (freshly renamed) Department for Education with a personal and well-informed commitment to his party's manifesto pledge to require the teaching of systematic, synthetic phonics. He started with a considerable policy advantage. The fact that the Rose Review had been commissioned and fully endorsed by a Labour Government meant that the Coalition Government was able to move forward on phonics with clear evidence that it was not a partisan issue, but had the support of all three main parties.

But Nick Gibb knew that a persistently stubborn attachment to mixed methods of word guessing was a major obstacle to making any improvement to reading standards and he believed that a whole series of different measures would be needed to ensure that schools received clear and consistent messages about the place of phonics in national policy. As a result he set about introducing a whole raft of measures to strengthen the framework of law, regulation and guidance around phonics. The changes he planned included a major strengthening of the place of phonics in the National Curriculum and the inclusion of an understanding of phonics in a set of reworked 'Teachers' Standards' (which lay down the minimum requirements for teachers' practice and conduct).

One of the first changes Nick Gibb introduced, was to increase the focus on the teaching of reading during Ofsted inspections. This required inspectors to pay particular attention to reading, particularly in Key Stage One. Amongst the changes was an expectation that inspectors' evidence gathering would include hearing children read – this had in the past been standard practice in inspections, but some years before it had been quietly abandoned. To support this change in the inspection framework all Ofsted inspectors were required to undertake some basic training in phonics. The significance that Ofsted was now attaching to phonics can be judged from the fact that this is the first and only time in which all Ofsted inspectors have been required to undergo training in a specific aspect of the curriculum.

Another of Nick Gibb's reforms was to require schools to publish on their websites information about the phonics programmes and reading schemes that they used. The intention was to ensure public access to key information about a school's policies and approaches to the teaching of reading.

The biggest change that Nick Gibb introduced was the requirement that an annual Phonics Screening Check should be administered to all children in Year 1 during the second half of the summer term. This Check is a simple tool to assess children's ability to use phonics to decode. Predictably its introduction was fiercely opposed by the teaching unions. In July 2012 the National Union of Teachers, the Association of Teachers and Lecturers and the National Association of Head Teachers carried out a joint survey of their members. Out of almost 3000 members who responded, 87% said that they thought the Phonics Screening Check should be discontinued. This resistance to checking on children's phonics progress is examined more fully later in this book.

The other major piece in the government's interlocking set of measures was a complete rewrite of the National Curriculum, including for the first time clear and unambiguous statements about the requirement to teach systematic, synthetic phonics.

This change, to be statutory from September 2014, will be the first time that phonics has been so explicitly required and after a hundred years of muddle in the teaching of reading, the new National Curriculum finally marks the end of official endorsement or toleration of the mixed methods of word guessing.

As well as measures to require schools to focus properly and effectively on phonics the Coalition Government also made a commitment to providing financial help for schools to fund additional spending needed to develop the teaching of phonics. This was implemented in the form of a match-funding for phonics scheme. A primary school could claim up to £3000 of government funding when it was matched by an equal spend from the school's own budget – so for example a school could buy materials costing £1000 for only £500 of its own money. Purchases had to be made from a catalogue in which all the items had been carefully evaluated by an expert to ensure that they met strict educational criteria.

The intention of this interlocking jigsaw of measures was to ensure improved professional understanding about phonics. The focus on reading by Ofsted, for example, was intended to ensure that schools had clear and objective feedback about their performance in teaching reading and to help them identify strengths and weaknesses in their practice. The inclusion of phonics within Teachers' Standards was intended to ensure that all teachers who needed it had up-to-date knowledge about the teaching of early reading. The Y1 Phonics Screening Check was intended to provide clear and unambiguous evidence to support an objective understanding of children's progress in decoding and to help schools in providing additional support for children who needed it. The changes to National Curriculum were intended to clear away decades of confusion so that schools could understand exactly what they needed to do.

But the Coalition Government was mistaken if it thought that all these measures to improve access to knowledge would secure a climate in which the ignorant and malicious war against phonics would come to an end. Schools proved stubbornly resistant to the prospect of improved understanding. For example, phonics training was included in the match-funding offer, but if schools used the match-funding scheme at all they used it mainly to buy books and teaching resources. A 2012/13 survey of nearly one thousand schools carried out by the National Foundation for Educational Research found only three schools that had used match-funding to ensure that staff were properly trained. Ironically, that same NFER report made clear the widespread confusion and misunderstanding about phonics amongst the teachers surveyed. Improvements in teachers' professional understanding were clearly urgently needed but these needs were not being recognised by the teachers themselves or by their headteachers.

The evidence of climate change around phonics suggests that if anything the level of anti-phonics hysteria has intensified in the last few years. Myths, misunderstandings and downright falsehoods not only persist but proliferate. And since the Rose Report and the Coalition Government's reforms, one myth has assumed particular prominence – an accusation that phonics is the enemy of comprehension.

10

The Simple View of Reading

In 1990 two American reading researchers, Wesley Hoover and Philip Gough, published a paper on *'The Simple View of Reading'*. In essence their paper described the reading process as being dependent on two separate things – decoding and language comprehension.

It should be noted that the name *'Simple View of Reading'* does not indicate that reading is to be thought of as a simple process. It is of course complex. The Simple View of Reading is 'simple' only in the same sense that a map is a simplification of a complex geo-physical reality. The authors express it this way: *"The simple view does not deny that the reading process is complex...The simple view simply holds that these complexities can be divided into two parts."*

The first part of the process – decoding – is misleadingly labelled in some versions of the 'Simple View' as 'Word Recognition'. But Hoover and Gough consistently refer to this dimension of reading as 'decoding' because for children learning to read, the word recognition process depends on the use of phonics.

The second part of the reading process is language comprehension, which Philip Gough succinctly defines as *"understanding those words once you have recognised them"*. This means of course not only understanding individual words, but understanding words in combination – phrases, sentences, paragraphs and so on.

One of the major pieces of evidence for the 'Simple View' is that these two abilities – decoding and comprehension – do not always or necessarily develop in a synchronised way. The fact that they can be disassociated has been verified by research but is also easily observable in everyday life. For example, almost every teacher has encountered a child with high verbal abilities – able to understand and use quite sophisticated language, able to listen with understanding to quite complex or subtle stories – but who is unable to read competently for themselves. These are children who have developed well on only one dimension of the Simple View of Reading – the dimension of language comprehension.

Conversely there are children who can decode well, but do not necessarily understand what they are reading. Children who are acquiring English as an additional language can find themselves in this situation, because they can acquire the phonic skills to 'crack the code' of English but may meet words on the page that are not yet within their spoken vocabulary. Any one of us, even fluent English speakers and readers, can find ourselves in the same situation if given some very complex text to read - for example a passage from Bertrand Russell's *Inquiry into Meaning and Truth*. We would probably have no trouble decoding the text – but comprehending what was meant would be hidden from all of us except those whose background knowledge enabled them to understand Russell's terminology and to follow his arguments.

Of course children who do not have the ability to decode the words on the page – to be able to work out what words the black squiggles on the page are representing – will not be able to comprehend the text at all, no matter how good their language comprehension might be. This might seem so obvious as not to need mentioning, but as we will see later in this book some opponents of phonics are blind to the obvious and appear to believe that children can understand a written text for themselves without being able to decode the words within it.

The plain implication of the 'Simple View of Reading' is that teaching must attend to both its parts. Phonics must be taught well and systematically so that children can be enabled to develop an eventual fluency with decoding. And teachers must work to develop and extend children's language – particularly through activities such as listening to good stories and talking about new words and their meanings.

The *Simple View of Reading* provides such an important framework for the teaching of phonics that an extensive outline of it was included in the *Rose Report*. The importance and significance of the *Simple View* has been routinely emphasised in almost all phonics training ever since.

The Simple View of Reading is more than just a theoretical framework – it is an immensely practical guide to teaching. That's why the revised National Curriculum for English, statutory from September 2014, embodies the *Simple View of Reading* in the organisation of its programmes of study which are structured under two headings, '*Word Reading*' and '*Comprehension*'. The wording of this new National Curriculum makes it clear that teaching must attend to both these dimensions. It also makes plain that the dimension of word reading requires the understanding that "*the letters on the page represent the sounds in spoken words*". So for the first time the alphabetic principle will be clearly embodied within the National Curriculum and, of equal significance, the importance of phonics will be explicitly linked to the importance of comprehension.

11

Lost for Words

"*In the beginning was the Word.*" Reading comprehension starts with words. Unless the 'squiggles on the page' can be decoded into the words they represent there is no possibility of comprehension. This might seem so obvious as not to need saying. But the critics of phonics will go to any lengths to deny what is obvious about comprehension.

As is made clear – in the Rose Report, in all high quality phonics training and in the new National Curriculum – reading with understanding is a product of phonics and language comprehension. Without the ability to decode children can comprehend spoken language and they can understand stories that are read to them, but they cannot read for themselves. Comprehension depends critically on being able to decode.

Professor Michael Pressley, one of the world's experts on reading comprehension, put it like this:

"Perhaps it is a truism, but students cannot understand texts if they cannot read the words. Before they can read the words, they have to be aware of the letters and the sounds represented by letters so that sounding out and blending of sounds can occur to pronounce words...Thus, a first recommendation to educators who want to improve students' comprehension skills is to teach them to decode well. Explicit instruction in sounding out words, which has been so well validated as helping many children to recognize words more certainly is a start in developing good comprehenders - but it is just a start. Word-recognition skills must be developed to the point of fluency if comprehension benefits are to be maximized."

The anti-phonics propaganda about comprehension is of three types. The first type is an assertion that those who advocate phonics ignore comprehension. In fact they usually go further and imply that teachers of phonics couldn't care less about comprehension.

No evidence is ever produced in support of this assertion. No phonics scheme is ever cited as being dismissive of comprehension. No teacher of phonics is ever produced who claims that comprehension is unimportant. None of the many hundreds of reading researchers who have demonstrated the importance of phonics is quoted as devaluing the importance of comprehension. The accusation is fraudulent.

Another line of false argument is that decoding inhibits comprehension – that it reduces children to 'barking at print'. This scenario – in which children can decode the words but do not understand what the text means – has been examined experimentally. Keith Stanovich, perhaps the most eminent reading researcher in the world, has this to say:

"There is no research evidence indicating that decoding a word into phonological form often takes place without meaning extraction, even in poor readers. To the contrary, a substantial body of evidence indicates that even for young children, word decoding automatically leads to semantic activation when the word is adequately established in memory."

Stanovich makes clear not only that decoding does not lead to 'barking at print' but also underlines a crucial implication of the Simple View of Reading – comprehension depends not only on phonics (to decode the words) but also on understanding language (to comprehend what the words mean). Good teachers attend to both. They ensure children gain mastery of the critical skills of phonics and consciously attend to developing and extending children's vocabulary.

A third line of attack is that phonics makes no difference – that being able to decode does not improve or even enable comprehension. This takes some swallowing. The proponents of this argument offer no clue as to how they think children can comprehend for themselves texts in which they cannot read the words.

These critics repeatedly stress the blindingly obvious – that reading is about deriving meaning. But they seem to believe that the meaning exists independently of the words and that children can somehow access this meaning without being able to read the words. The opponents of phonics completely fail to face the fact that eliciting meaning from a text is inevitably made harder when children struggle to decode.

A particular trick is to demand evidence that children who can decode are better at comprehending than children who cannot decode. The evidence exists: children who are poor at reading comprehension have been repeatedly shown to have poor word recognition skills. In an article for Scientific American in 2002, four leading researchers explained that teachers needed to "*recognise the ample evidence that youngsters who are directly taught phonics become better at reading, spelling and comprehension*".

63

But in their stubborn blindness to all the evidence, the critics completely ignore the obvious fact that a child cannot reasonably be expected to comprehend a text without being able to decode the words. As Keith Stanovich explains "*while it is possible for adequate word recognition skill to be accompanied by poor comprehension abilities, the converse virtually never occurs.*"

It is curious that phonics-deniers cling so obstinately to the argument about comprehension. The basic fact – that recognising the words represented by the squiggles on the page is essential to understanding print – is so self-evident that it provokes unbelief that anyone could argue to the contrary. But argue some do.

Recognising the fallacy of the 'children can comprehend without needing to decode' argument does not require special study. It does not need knowledge of the specialised literature of reading research. *Recognition that comprehension requires decoding is simple common sense.* As we shall see, it is the repeated gainsaying of common sense and evidence that points to the dark side of phonics denial.

12

Phonics First, Fast and Only

Well, there's partial phonics and there's systematic, synthetic phonics.

Partial phonics has been used for years not as a universal strategy for decoding words but as one of the 'clues' to support guessing. This often took the form of using the initial 'sound' in a word to help narrow the choices down. Just one more clue in the old and futile guessing game.

Another variant of partial phonics was to teach clusters of letters as though they were fundamental units. So, for example, pairs of consonants were taught as individual 'clusters'. This is completely unnecessary because blending consecutive consonants is (apart from some special exceptions such as two letter graphemes called digraphs) no more than applying the skill of blending to each consonant in turn.

So treating consonant clusters as fundamental units was fundamentally misleading as well as inefficient. Acquiring phonics in this way was never

65

going to be more than partial because learning consonant clusters on a one-by-one basis would turn the phonics curriculum into a lifetime's journey.

Equally misleading and inefficient was another variation of partial phonics in which children were introduced to words broken down into sub-units known as onsets and rimes. These 'word-families' would all follow a similar pattern – e.g. tap, cap, nap, etc. A teacher surveyed in the *Effective Teachers of Literacy Project*, towards the end of the 1990s described some group work using this approach: "*We've done –og words – we did that last week and the week before and we're onto –at words.*"

Another tactic in partial phonics was to teach a few phonics 'rules' – e.g. "*When two vowels go walking the first one does the talking.*" Another and very common rule was known as '*magic e*'. Teaching like this was always partial phonics because it amounted to a ragbag of so-called rules the application of which was always uncertain, unreliable and incomplete.

Children who learned to use partial phonics as one 'clue' within the mixed methods of guessing were being encouraged to look for help in every direction except the critical one – the full sequence of letters within a word. In contrast, systematic, synthetic phonics sets out to enable children to make full use of the alphabetic principle and to be confident to tackle every unknown word using phonics, not partially but fully all the way through the word. The term 'systematic, synthetic phonics' has come to be used in order to make clear this difference to the old-style partial phonics.

Systematic, synthetic phonics has as its backbone a 'road-map' of all the grapheme-phoneme correspondences to be taught. As previously explained, these are usually broken down into two stages – the first stage teaches the simple code and in the second stage children are taught the complex code. This means that children are introduced not to just a few odds and ends of phonic knowledge but are given a full, working knowledge of how letters and combinations of letters are typically used to represent the phonemes in English spelling. A good systematic, synthetic phonics programme sets out the order in which all the phonic knowledge should be taught. Children are never overwhelmed by the complexity and extent of all that will have to be eventually learned because their working knowledge is built up gradually, step by step.

The expectation is that systematic, synthetic phonics teaching will start when children begin in the reception class. In some nurseries and play groups children are introduced to a preliminary stage that is about developing children's sensitivity to the sounds within words. Not all pre-school settings do this but the key part of this work is also included from the start of systematic, synthetic phonics teaching so children will be able to start phonics at the beginning of reception even if they have not experienced this preliminary stage.

The plan of systematic, synthetic phonics teaching is that it should progress at a good pace. In broad terms the intention is that by the end of the reception year (or slightly sooner) children should have been introduced to the simple code and by the end of Year 1 children should have been taught the complex code. The expectation is that by the end of Key Stage One (Year 2) children should have become confident in their use of phonics to decode and have become successful readers able to read confidently and accurately books and other texts for their age group. We will look more closely at this pace of teaching later in this book.

Because of these two principles – a prompt start at the beginning of reception and the aim of securing successful reading by the end of Key Stage One – systematic, synthetic phonics is sometimes characterised as *'phonics first and fast'*.

The intention of systematic, synthetic phonics is, of course, that children will come to understand the alphabetic principle and will become able to apply their growing phonic knowledge and skills to decoding words all the way through from left to right. In this approach the letters in words come to be seen as what they are – a representation of the sounds we hear in that word when it spoken. When children hesitate over a word, teachers of systematic, synthetic phonics are not expected to direct children to seek alternative clues – such as guessing from a picture or from context – because it is confusing (and misleading) to distract children from the key skill of decoding.

Because word-guessing is not part of systematic, synthetic phonics the principle *'phonics first and fast'* is sometimes cited as *'phonics first, fast and only'*. It's important to note that 'only' is used in that description to make it clear that phonics is not being advocated as just one of a set of mixed methods of word guessing. Phonics *'only'* means no teaching or encouragement of word guessing. Those hostile to phonics are happy to seize on 'phonics only' and to misrepresent 'only' as implying that there is nothing more to reading than decoding. A related form of this myth is to claim that phonics alone is being represented as a 'magic bullet'.

These expectations – first, fast (and only) – have made their way into the new National Curriculum for

English, but they are not new. The same expectations are clearly set out in the phonics programme *Letters and Sounds*. That phonics scheme, written for and published by the DfES in the wake of the Rose Review, was distributed free to all primary schools in England in 2008. More than five years later it is believed to be the phonics programme most widely used in this country.

The principle of 'first, fast and only' is clearly expressed in *Letters and Sounds*, through its Notes of Guidance and through the structure and progression of the programme's content. For example, the guidance states that children should be "*focused on decoding rather than on the use of unreliable strategies such as looking at the illustrations, rereading the sentence, saying the first sound and guessing what might fit*".

However, although *Letters and Sounds* has been very widely adopted (perhaps because it was free) there has clearly been widespread resistance to its underlying principle of 'first, fast and only'. The National Union of Teachers has issued this advice to its members: "*Phonics alone will not produce fluent readers. In order to become fluent and accurate readers children must learn to use all of the cueing systems together.*" The NAS/UWT, which claims to be the largest teaching union in the country, has announced that a survey of its members showed that "*89 per cent asserted that they needed to use a combination of cues such as context, initial letter sounds and/or illustrations to make meaning from text*". A survey carried out by Sheffield Hallam University in 2011 found that 74% of nearly 300 primary schools surveyed claimed that they encouraged pupils to use a range of cueing systems, such as context or picture clues, as well as phonics.

This stubborn clinging to the old mixed methods of word guessing is more than just a persistence of professional habit. It is a persistence of expectation. Expectation that reading standards are not just '*as they are*' but '*as they should be*'. Perpetuating the traditional methods of the teaching of reading inevitably perpetuates the traditional gap that marginalises and excludes those who struggle to read and never learn to do so successfully.

In 1998 the government appointed a working group under the chairmanship of Sir Claus Moser to investigate adult basic skills. The group gathered evidence that showed that about one in five adults had low skills of literacy. Around 6% of the adult working population were found to have literacy skills that were so low that they were "*likely to have great difficulty with any reading, struggling to read the simplest and shortest texts.*" A further 13% had

71

reading skills so limited that they could only read "*slowly with little understanding*".

This exclusion from effective literacy of around 20% of the population is an inevitable outcome of the muddled and incoherent methods that have characterised the teaching of reading in England for at least a hundred years. The resistance to '*phonics first, fast and only*' is resistance to the only practicable means of putting an end to the process that has relentlessly turned out around one in twenty as a literacy 'have-not'. If we go on doing what we have always done, we will go on getting what we have always got.

13

Reading by Six

The pace and progression implied by 'phonics first and fast' embodies the idea that the teaching of phonics should be *time-limited*. The intention is that if the full complex code can be taught by the end of Year 1, then children are able to go on to consolidate and reinforce their knowledge and skills to the point where decoding becomes automatic. The sooner children are able to read well for themselves the better, not least because independence in reading enables children to read more satisfyingly, more fully, more widely – and with greater enjoyment. Professor Keith Stanovitch puts it like this: *"Children who quickly develop efficient decoding processes find reading enjoyable because they can concentrate on the meaning of the text read. They read more in school and of equal importance, reading becomes a self-chosen activity for them. "*

One of the first moves made by the Coalition Government to establish its commitment to phonics was to commission an Ofsted report on the characteristics of primary schools that are very successful in teaching reading. The schools focused on in the resulting report represented a range in terms of ethnicity and socio-economic backgrounds. Each school had been judged to be outstanding in their most recent inspection. In each school the very great majority of children achieved at least level 2b by the end of Key Stage One. The report concluded that "*The diligent, concentrated and systematic teaching of phonics is central to the success of all the schools that achieve high reading standards in Key Stage 1.*" Its endorsement of 'phonics first and fast' was clearly reflected in the report's title, *Reading by Six*.

Reading by Six made clear that "*phonics is an indispensable tool for children to make sense of written words*" and near the beginning of the report is a penetrating observation that comes close to the heart of the case developed in this book: "*The schools in this survey have two things in common: the belief that every child can learn to read and the strategies to make this happen.*" This linking of the schools' high expectations with their central focus on phonics is a key insight. It is well-known that those who advocate and support the teaching of systematic, synthetic phonics are openly and explicitly committed to raising standards of reading, and in particular committed to ensuring that those who are currently left behind in reading are given the teaching they need to succeed. This is a very different position from those who oppose phonics.

A notable feature of the anti-phonics position in general is that it routinely avoids any reference to standards, let alone any suggestion that they need to improve. If anti-phonics campaigners mention standards of reading at all it is often only to insist that there is nothing to worry about. Reading standards they like to say are an imaginary crisis, part of a 'rhetoric of decline'. These critics of phonics, all capable and confident readers themselves, show no concern for those who are excluded from the privileged world of reading. According to a statistical briefing issued by the National Literacy Trust, one in six people in the UK struggle with literacy. Systematic, synthetic phonics is promoted by those who care passionately about that struggle and are determined to put an end to it. Anti-phonics propagandists campaign aggressively against the prospect.

14

The Phonics Screening Check

In 2010 the Coalition Government published a White Paper, *The Importance of Teaching*, which set out the broad lines of education ambition and policy. This included a commitment to "*introducing a simple reading check at age six to guarantee that children have mastered the basic skills of early reading and also ensure we can identify those with learning difficulties*".

The proposal of a check on phonic decoding had been around for some time and under the previous Labour Government, the suggestion had met with some sympathy at the most senior level amongst officials. But the idea was out of the question at the political level. During the life of the Labour Government successive Secretaries of State for Education had found themselves on the rack over assessment outcomes and there was no appetite for further punishment.

During the last years in opposition, Nick Gibb had been convinced by the argument for a phonics check and he had ensured that it was included in the 2010 Conservative Party Manifesto. So the announcement in the Coalition Government's White Paper came as no surprise. Work was immediately put in hand for a pilot run of the Check in 2011 and it was introduced as a statutory requirement in time for it to be used with all Y1 children in the summer term of 2012.

On the face of it the structure of the Check was straightforward and unexceptional. It consisted of a list of forty separate words. The Check was administered on a one-to-one basis with a teacher noting each child's response. Thirty-two words out of forty was established as the threshold. This standard was agreed by the groups of teachers involved in the piloting of the Check.

The use of a list of words to check children's reading progress has been routine in schools for many years. Many schools have used standardised lists of these words as a well-known means of establishing a score known as a reading age. Educational psychologists also use word-reading lists as one of the measures by which they check on reading achievement. The use of individual words was, however, seized on by anti-phonics protesters who insisted that the ability to read individual words meant nothing.

77

The aspect of the Phonics Check that aroused most hostility was the inclusion of pseudo-words, sometimes called non-words or even 'nonsense words'. These are made-up words that conform with regular orthography but have been specifically invented to use for assessment purposes. The utility of such words for assessment has been well-established for years.

Research has shown that the early ability to read pseudo-words is strongly associated with later success in reading. The reason for this is simple. Children who can decode a wide range of pseudo-words are clearly demonstrating that they have cracked, or are well on the way to cracking, the phonic code – that is using knowledge of the relationships between letters and sounds and the skill of blending to tackle any word they come across. They are not relying on a visual memory of the word nor are they guessing the word. And of course fluent reading depends on this ability to decode any word that happens to come along.

So non-words were included in the Y1 Phonics Screening Check because they help to provide a clear and unambiguous picture of children's knowledge and skill. If a child can decode one of these pseudo-words their success cannot be explained away as just a word they happened to recognise or remember.

Helpfully, the Check is designed in such a way as to make it quite clear to children which of the words they are being asked to read are pseudo-words.

The value of pseudo-words has been well-established for years – long before the Y1 Phonics Screening Check. The widely used *Letters and Sounds* phonics programme (probably the most widely used programme in the country) refers to the use of these words and provides examples. High quality commercial phonics programme also make use of pseudo-words for assessment. The point is frequently made that '*every word is a nonsense word until you know what it means*' and children who cannot use phonics skills to decode pseudo-words have little or no chance of enlarging their vocabulary through encountering in print real words that were not previously in their spoken vocabulary.

Pseudo-words were included in the Y1 Phonics Screening Check because of the penetrating light they can throw on children's phonics progress but this feature of the Check met with strident hostility from those opposed to phonics. Their objections ranged from the absurd (that children were being 'taught nonsense') to the downright deceitful (that children who did not reach the threshold on the Check had to be told that they had 'failed').

A further line of attack was developed by Y1 teachers who claimed that the Check was misleading because many good readers were unable to read at least 32 of the words. But the plain fact is that children who have not reached the expected standard on the check are not good readers, not yet – they may enjoy stories, they may have learned to recognise a small stock of words by sight, they may have good vocabularies and they may have learned the stories and rhymes in some books by heart; but they are not yet good readers, because they don't yet have the range of phonic knowledge and skills to decode unfamiliar words.

The Check was deliberately constructed to be relatively unchallenging. Of the forty words in the 2012 Check only six words required phonic knowledge that might not be expected to be taught until Y1. So thirty-four of the words should have been decodable by the end of the reception year. In terms of *Letters and Sounds* (still, for now, the phonics programme most commonly used), two words could be read by the end of Phase 2, a further 16 words by the end of Phase 3 and 16 more by the end of Phase 4. These phases are all reception work. Only 6 words in the entire Check come from Phase 5, which is for Y1.

Despite the 2012 Check being deliberately set at an unchallenging level, the national outcomes were far from reassuring. Nationally just 58% of children were able to read at least thirty two of the forty words. And under examination even this figure turned out to be an over-statement. When *Ofqual* (the regulatory authority whose remit is to maintain standards and confidence in qualifications) examined the outcomes for the Check they saw a tell-tale 'spike' at the threshold point of 32 words correctly decoded. Ofqual expressed their findings delicately but plainly: *"The distribution of scores awarded by teachers is significantly skewed... for example, almost five times as many pupils attained 32 marks (the threshold) as attained 31 marks."* In other words there was a widespread massaging of the figures to give children a score higher than they should have received.

Perhaps some of the teachers who falsified the outcomes in this way were influenced by a particularly poisonous myth spread by the anti-phonics movement. This myth insisted that children who did not reach the threshold on the Check had to be *"told that they had failed"*. The regulations accompanying the Check actually said something very different:

"Teachers must tell parents whether or not their child met the required standard to ensure they are

81

aware of their child's progress in developing phonics skills... Schools can use their judgement about the best method of communication with parents and may wish to include additional information such as how parents can support their child to progress with their phonics and reading at home."

This is so plain and so different from the allegation that children were to be told that they had *'failed'* that it is hard to escape the conclusion that this myth was concocted not just for the purpose of discrediting the Check, but in the hope of causing actual anxiety and harm to children.

The Check was roundly dismissed by the phonics objectors as not being a 'proper test of reading'. But it does not claim to be a 'Y1 Reading Test'. The name, *Y1 Phonics Screening Check*, makes it plain that it is specifically an instrument designed to focus clearly on strengths and weaknesses in children's phonics skills. It aims to provide a representation of the extent to which children are able to use phonic decoding to tackle words, including words they have not met before. If children cannot decode at least thirty two relatively simple words/non-words from the list then they have under-developed phonics skills and without further help and teaching of phonics will struggle to read independently.

The criticisms of the Check from the anti-phonics movement consist of misunderstandings, misrepresentation and downright deceit. The Y1 Phonics Screening Check is not a blunt or faulty instrument. It is intended to focus only on phonics – if teachers can learn to see through the myths spread by those opposed to phonics, then the Screening Check should also act to focus teachers' minds on the flaws in the hit or miss method of word guessing.

15

Decodable Readers

Many adults have memories – sometimes affectionate, sometimes not – of the reading schemes used in their primary schools. The nostalgic value that these can have is demonstrated by the way in which the images from the *Ladybird* scheme, which began publication in 1964, have today achieved a brand and merchandising status in their own right.

The history of reading schemes makes for a fascinating study, but despite significant improvements over the years in the way in which these books have been produced, the overall educational judgement has to be that most of the reading schemes traditionally used in primary schools have colluded with and reinforced the haphazard mixed methods of word-guessing.

Of course it is to be expected that the publishers of reading schemes will set out to produce material to meet commercial demand. If schools want to teach word-guessing then publishers are likely to design their reading schemes accordingly. But reading schemes do not only 'follow the market'. They can also set out to influence the practice of teaching and the record shows that this influence has generally been on the side of mixed methods, with some partial phonics thrown in.

For example, the introduction to the *Happy Venture* reading scheme, widely used in England from the 1930s right through to the 1970, clearly nailed its flag to the mast of mixed methods: *"This series of Readers is the result of extensive experiment, and combines the merits of both the phonic and sentence methods of teaching reading. To allow the child to make full use of content and to develop a normal eye-span, so necessary for fluency and comprehension, the approach is made primarily from the stand-point of the sentence-method; but the importance of phonics is given due recognition."*

A later example, the Ladybird books (strictly speaking the *Key Words Reading Scheme*) began to appear in 1964. It had as its basis the look-and-say method of recognising words by sight. Children were expected to build a visual lexical memory through frequent repetition of a stock of 'keywords'.

More recently, the *Oxford Reading Tree* scheme, which began to appear in 1985, was described by its publishers as a departure from the *"traditional look-*

and-say schemes of the time" but Joyce Morris has pointed out the phonics resources originally published with the scheme were described as 'optional'.

Reading schemes are specifically designed and marketed to help children to learn to read. But no wonder teachers persisted with mixed methods when their classrooms were stocked with scheme books that relied on memorising whole-words, expected children to guess words from context, to identify words from a picture clue or encouraged them to rely on their oral memory to supply frequently repeated phrases.

But now there is a new kind of reading scheme available. These schemes are made up of books that are described as *decodable readers*. These books use only words that children can decode using just the phonics they have been taught so far. The sequence of decodable books is matched to the sequence of phonics teaching laid out in one or other of the phonics teaching programmes, so that at every stage there is a selection of books available that enable children to practise and apply what they have learned so far. As more and more phonics is taught so the progression in the decodable readers advances, enabling the books to use an ever-widening vocabulary.

The advantage of these decodable readers is three-fold. Firstly they enable children to experience success as they are able to use what they have learned in order to read confidently and independently. Secondly, these books do not encourage habits of word guessing because they can be read using just what the children have been taught so far. The third advantage is that these books help children to develop and have confidence in the concept of the alphabetic principle. They can see that phonics works and this encourages them to make further progress with phonics in the certain knowledge that it will bring them increasing success in their reading. As children's phonic knowledge progresses so more and more words become decodable and so the need for carefully designed readers will drop away. By some time into Year 1 most children should be able to tackle with confidence any book appropriate for their age range, whether it has been designed as decodable or not.

Inevitably the opponents of phonics are violently opposed to the use of decodable books. Their arguments are based on misconceptions, mistakes or inventions. For example one widely-circulated myth is that the use of decodable books means that children must not have access to any other books. This is completely untrue. In schools that teach phonics

87

first, fast and only children are surrounded by books and children are encouraged to browse amongst them and enjoy them. The decodable readers are there specifically to provide books that children can use to practise their phonic learning. These are books that children and their teachers can expect to be capable of being read independently. No one who properly understands systematic, synthetic phonics holds that children should be denied access to books that contain words they cannot yet decode.

Another argument from the anti-phonics camp is that decodable readers are inevitably artificial, contrived and intrinsically uninteresting and motivating. These are criticisms that have also been made in the past against the language used in non-decodable reading schemes (*"This is Dick. Run, Dick, Run."*) but the reality is that the quality of writing of all reading schemes has improved markedly in the last twenty or thirty years and decodable readers conform to the contemporary expectation that reading scheme books will be written to a high standard. One set of decodable books has even been written by Julia Donaldson, author of the best-selling book *The Gruffalo* and a former children's laureate.

Decodable texts are so valuable that the new National Curriculum for English, statutory from September 2014, will require all primary schools to have them. As long as teachers can discard or discount the errors and inventions of the anti-phonics movement, then the use of decodable readers alongside good effective teaching of phonics will enable unprecedented numbers of children to experience successful, confident reading.

16

"I was never taught phonics but I still learned to read"

Another of the weapons used against phonics is to point out that there are many adult readers who were never taught phonics. This proves, according to this argument, that learning phonics is unnecessary.

Whilst adults may have unreliable memories of how they were taught when they were very young, it is very likely – given the long history of muddled teaching of reading – that many adult readers were never taught phonics, or at least were taught only bits and pieces of 'partial phonics'.

The first thing to note about the '*I learned to read without phonics*' argument is that it assumes that these readers do not have phonics, or do not use it to read. An alternative explanation (and as we shall see the correct one) is that adult readers are simply unaware of using phonics, unconscious of the part it plays in what has become a well-established, possibly fluent, process. The intention of teaching phonics to children is, after all, to enable them in time to apply the decoding process automatically and unconsciously.

A consequence of automatic decoding is that readers inevitably are no longer consciously aware of how their reading happens. For example, a fluent reader's impression of their reading is likely to be that it is not based on letter by letter analysis of the words. But research shows that this impression is inaccurate. The scientific evidence points unmistakeably to the fact that skilled readers do not take in whole words as single units but thoroughly process the individual letters in the words they read.

Fluent readers are likely to be similarly unaware that their reading depends on a process of mentally 'sounding out' albeit at an unconscious level. But research has shown this to be the case. For example, in one experiment, carried out by Professor Guy Van Orden, skilled readers were first asked a question – e.g. "*Is this a flower?*" and were then shown a word that was a homophone for a correct answer – e.g. "*Rows*". Those participating in the experiment frequently mistook the homophone for a correct answer, revealing that they were automatically using phonics to decode the word and then accessing an (in this case incorrect) meaning.

Another source of the myth that skilled readers do not use phonics has emerged from the creation of puzzles in which some simple and familiar text is 'recoded' into non-alphabetic symbols. Skilled readers can often make a good job of tackling this puzzle and are often able to reconstruct the text from its coded form. In fact this activity gives a misleading impression of the reading process, because skilled readers bring to the challenge an enormous amount of explicit and tacit knowledge about things such as letter patterns, word length, vowel/consonant frequencies, and so on. This knowledge can help them to solve the cryptic puzzle, but can mislead them into thinking that phonics is irrelevant to their own reading.

So those who argue "*I was never taught phonics but I learned to read*" are mistaken if they think they have not acquired phonic knowledge and skills. The question then boils down to how they can have learned these things in the absence of any or much direct teaching.

The answer is that many children are able to self-teach, that is to fathom out by their own efforts (not necessarily consciously) the relationship between letters and the sounds in words and are able to 'crack the code' from what they have perceived. These children have discovered the alphabetic principle for themselves without any (or much) phonics teaching.

This ability to self-teach will of course be present even when children are directly taught phonics. In fact self-teaching gets an additional boost in those circumstances because it explicitly exposes the alphabetic principle and this helps to provide a focus for children's self-teaching.

It is clear that some children are able to transcend the limitations of teaching that avoids or minimises the importance of phonics. Some will learn to read fluently. Others will learn to read well enough to get by. But others, who are not able to work out the code and internalise it for themselves, will fall by the wayside. We know that without direct teaching of phonics it is disadvantaged children that are particularly (though not exclusively) at risk.

But if despite mixed methods of word guessing *some* children can still learn to read well enough, why teach phonics to *all* children? Part of the answer is that we cannot predict which children will be able to make good progress despite poor teaching (even advantaged children are not guaranteed a free pass) and if we are to maximise children's life chances we have to ensure that they all receive the best teaching that can be provided.

Another reason for ensuring that all children get explicit teaching about the alphabetic principle is that it makes an important contribution to the development of accurate spelling. Learning to spell well requires more than phonics, but an understanding of the alphabetic principle and the complex code is an important underpinning to the knowledge that leads to accurate spelling.

The *2013 CBI/Pearson Education and Skills Survey* found that 32% of employers reported dissatisfaction with the basic literacy standards among school and college leavers. When surveys like this appear they are sometimes met with an attempt to discount them with the retort that there is a long history, going back to at least the 1920s, of employers complaining about the standard of school leavers. One critic dismisses contemporary reports of employer concerns as part of the "*long moan of history*". But when you take into account the evidence that the muddled and ineffective methods of word guessing have been the standard approach to reading in our schools for so many successive generations it is hardly surprising to find long-standing and persisting concerns. The fact that some children are fortunate enough to survive the muddled methods of word guessing and learn how to read without the explicit teaching of phonics is no reason for sticking stubbornly to the methods that condemn so many to failure.

17

Myths, misconceptions and downright
deceptions

The scrutiny of anti-phonics argument does not make for a broad field of study. What appears to be a long list of misunderstandings and inventions actually separates, under analysis, into two distinct groups. One category of criticisms sets out to undermine or even deny the alphabetic principle. The other line of attack is to assert that phonics teaching carries dangers and disadvantages and even causes harm.

The idea that the letters in words represent the sounds we hear in those words when they are spoken comes frequently under attack from the critics of phonics. What's striking about this kind of argument is how commonly the attempts to demolish the alphabetic principle actually contain their own refutation – such as the arguments that use invented spelling to make their point. For example, a letter to the Times Educational Supplement attempted to 'debunk' phonics by making its point sarcastically in invented spelling – "*inglish is afta orl baysikly a fonikly structured langwij*". But this letter conceded the very point it was trying to attack. We could understand this letter because we know that letters in words are used to represent the sounds we hear in those words and we can use our phonic knowledge to read it because it is written using phonemically plausible spelling.

A related line of argument runs something like this: "*I can read German but I don't understand a word of it. This proves that phonics is a waste of time*". It's hard to understand why this argument was thought to pass muster on its first outing, but many critics of phonics must have had the syllogism-bypass operation because it keeps on being repeated. The argument is self-defeating. German is being read because it is being decoded. A familiarity with the sound-spelling system in German is necessary before the letters of the alphabet can be translated into the sounds they represent. The second point it concedes is equally basic to the case for systematic, synthetic phonics. Phonics is essential but not sufficient: fluency in decoding needs to be accompanied by language comprehension. This is the Simple View of Reading.

Very commonly the attack on the alphabetic principle makes use of the obvious fact that in

English the same letter (or group of letters) can represent more than one sound. A common example used by the critics of phonics is that the letter '*a*' in the word *cat*, represents a different sound from the same letter in the word '*was*'. It is implied that this makes phonics unusable, when in fact the aim of systematic, synthetic phonics is in a step-by-step and logical way, to enable children to understand this complexity and use their knowledge to tackle unknown words with confidence. But the argument carries inherently its own rebuttal. These critics are able to give examples of the complex code in action, because they understand it. They know that the same letters can represent different sounds; they are well aware of those complexities and can readily supply examples. This is the very same phonics knowledge that they claim either does not exist or should not be learned.

A variation on this line of argument is to assert that there are hundreds of letter-sound correspondences to learn (461 is a figure often quoted) and that the sheer number of these demonstrates the impossibility of them all being learned let alone being applied in reading. Those using this argument sometimes seem to believe that there are 461 ways of decoding any word but in any event the aim of phonics is not to teach any and every possible letter-sound correspondence. The aim is to give children a functional use of phonics that will enable them to read confidently, independently and successfully. For example it is not necessary to teach young children how to decode words that use *ps* to represent the /s/ phoneme (as in words like 'psephology' and 'psoriasis'). One study, at the University of Warwick, showed that even just 60 grapheme-phoneme correspondences were "highly useful". A typical systematic, synthetic phonics programme will set out to teach rather more than that – about 100 but still far less than the figure of 461 frequently cited by phonics critics.

The critics who make so much of the amount of phonics that needs to be learned noticeably avoid describing the impossible mountain of learning that their rejection of phonics implies in its place. Hundreds of words would have to be learned by sight – the Dolch Sight-Word List contains 315 words alone and this list (compiled in the 1940s) only claimed to cover around 75% of the words used in children's books of the time. The Fry's Instant Word List, compiled in the 1990s, is even longer - it contains a thousand words. Even this is only the beginning of the challenge. There are, for example, estimated to be about 8000 different words in just the average copy of a low-end tabloid newspaper. How much effort would have had to be expended to acquire all or most of these words by sight or in trying to guess each word from clues? Come to that how much effort would have to put into deciding which clue was the right one to follow? Compared to all this wasteful, inefficient and ineffectual effort, learning phonics seems a very small matter.

When they are not trying to undermine the alphabetic principle, the critics produce a long list of imaginary disadvantages to phonics as a teaching method. Many of these have already been dealt with in this book. For example the allegation that children learning phonics are not allowed access to real books or that phonics teaching ignores or even dismisses the importance of comprehension.

Another of these trumped-up charges is that teaching phonics condemns children to dull, repetitive, formal 'drill' administered by unimaginative teachers. No evidence is ever produced to justify the idea that phonics makes inevitably for teaching that is boring and uninteresting. Those who have any experience of watching good phonics teaching know how false this suggestion is. As Sir Jim Rose pointed out in a letter to the Guardian: *"There is plenty of evidence to show that children find high-quality phonic work rewarding and derive great satisfaction from taking part in the activities it presents to achieve the goal of reading."*

Closely behind this 'phonics teaching is dull' myth comes the accusation that teaching phonics ignores the importance of reading for pleasure. It is never explained by these critics why learning to decode should turn children against reading for pleasure. In fact there is an obvious connection between teaching phonics and the development of a personal appetite for reading. The personal sense of reading independently for pleasure is just pie-in-the-sky if you are a child who has never been enabled to crack the code.

Sometimes the argument seems to concede that phonics may 'suit' some children but is not appropriate for all because of individual differences in something called *'learning styles'*. The notion that children have an innate or acquired dominant style of learning - the visual, auditory and kinaesthetic styles are the usual candidates but there are others – has been shown time and time again to be a baseless myth.

A particularly perverse form of this myth leads to the idea that some things should simply not be taught to all children. This seems to be what at least some anti-phonics campaigners are thinking of when they argue that children learn to read 'in different ways'. Christine Blower, General Secretary of the NUT, may have had this in mind when she said, "*Children have different learning styles and develop at different ages and stages, a fact that the phonics check does not recognise.*"

The simplest response to this line of attack is that phonics is not a teaching style but a body of specific knowledge or content (grapheme-phoneme correspondences) and two skills (blending and segmenting). Learning styles, to borrow a phrase from Gilbert and Sullivan, "have nothing to do with the case".

When one anti-phonics argument after another turns out to be baseless and misinformed it is easy to see that there is no case to argue. But any propaganda will thrive if it is repeated loudly and frequently enough - and anti-phonics propaganda is no exception. These arguments spread on the internet through websites and social media; the inventions are repeated in teacher training institutions by ill-informed or ideologically-motivated lecturers and tutors; the myths find an easy outlet in the press too, from the *Socialist Worker* to the *Guardian* and the *Daily Express*. Even the *Times Educational Supplement*, a weekly magazine to be found in practically every school staffroom, has become a regular mouthpiece for cynical and ill-informed teachers' malicious slurs on phonics. Perhaps this is what the editor of the *Times Educational Supplement* had in mind when, on his retirement in 2013, he wrote a final editorial containing a bitter warning against teachers representing themselves as a *"sullen, whingeing, down-at-heel trade."*

Much of the propaganda is passed on by people who have blindly accepted the myths and inventions without troubling to check for themselves. Not that many of these inventions require extensive research to expose their falsity – many of them are so obviously illogical and self-contradictory that they could only be accepted by those who want to believe in the conclusion and are not too worried about how they got there.

However blindly these myths and misconceptions have come to be accepted, people are still responsible for their own opinions – and responsible too for the consequences or implications of those opinions. Those who invent anti-phonics propaganda and those who pass it on (however blindly) are collectively erecting a defensive bulwark around reading standards that are plainly too low and setting out to thwart a well-informed and concentrated effort to extend literacy to those currently left behind. Anti-phonics propaganda is not an innocent pursuit.

18

The Matthew Effect

"*For unto every one that hath shall be given, and he
shall have abundance: but from him that hath not
shall be taken away even that which he hath.*"

These well-known words, from the *Gospel
According to Matthew*, provided the starting point for
a theory developed in the late 1960s by the American
sociologist Robert K Merton. He coined the term
'Matthew Effect' to describe what he identified as a
bias in the way in which scientific recognition is given
disproportionately to those who are already eminent
while less well-known scientists receive less
recognition for work of similar significance. In
Merton's view the 'Matthew Effect' tended in a
number of ways to give disproportionate advantage to
those scientists who were already advantaged by their
reputation and worked negatively to reduce the credit
given to lesser-known scientists who did work of
equal importance.

This idea of a Matthew Effect was taken up by
others and its application investigated in different

fields, including education. The research proved fruitful. A range of situations – social and economic – were found in which the Matthew Effect could be identified or demonstrated. Put simply the investigations showed that initial advantage frequently bestowed a supplementary bonus. There is a kind of 'advantage dividend' available – those who are able to get 'ahead of the game' get an additional reward simply from having first put their nose in front.

Before long the Matthew Effect was found in children's reading development. It works like this: Children who learn to read well then proceed to read more than those of their peers who are still struggling to read. The advantaged read faster and are able to read in a more sustained way. They are able to enjoy books that are more rewarding – for example they can read books with more complex story lines and that contain more challenging vocabulary that is new to the readers. Their reading development progresses at an increasingly fast pace, because they are able to 'practise' their reading skills more frequently and more thoroughly and because the amount and kind of reading material they encounter enhances their reading knowledge and ability.

Meanwhile, those whose reading development is more problematic fall further and further behind.

Because reading is difficult they read more slowly and so they practise less. They read less in quantity. The opportunity to encounter new words and expand their vocabulary is reduced. Because reading is frustrating they have less appetite for reading and so they choose to read less often.

In this way the gap between the less and the more capable readers not only opens up but continually widens. The 'advantage dividend' accelerates the progress of the more successful while the others fall increasingly far behind. The difference in something as simple as the number of words read in a week bestows a cumulative and accelerating advantage on those who read better and consequently read more. The variety of those words and the greater number of newly-encountered words conveys yet more advantage.

Children who begin school with a reading advantage – the ones most likely to benefit from the Matthew Effect – are those who have come from homes where reading is clearly valued and supported. In these homes children are much more likely to have been surrounded by books, to have been given books of their own, to have been taken to the local library and to have been read to regularly and repeatedly. These children have been primed for reading in a way that makes it much more likely that they can make the best of the muddled teaching of mixed methods with, if they are lucky, partial phonics thrown in. They are potentially able to rise above the limitations of their teaching and gradually to crack the alphabetic code for themselves. These children are the lucky ones and the Matthew Effect will ensure that their head start will give them an enduring and increasing advantage.

Of course the Matthew Effect can never be eliminated. Even on an entirely level playing field some will pull ahead of the others. Well-to-do professionals and the middle class in general have a proven track record of taking every opportunity available to secure, maintain and improve their social, educational and economic advantage. But to withhold or deny *phonics first, fast and only* is to accelerate and add injustice to the negative cycle of disadvantage.

19

The Literacy Club

Within a few miles of each other, seeded through the most affluent parts of town, stand the prestigious clubs of London – the Athenaeum, the Carlton, the Reform, Boodles and so on – of which membership is, for many, still an avidly sought mark of status. These clubs are aloof, mysterious and, above everything else, *exclusive.*

Anthony Samson, that legendary anatomist of the British establishment, wrote of these places: "*The point of a club is not who it lets in, but who it keeps out*".

In the nineteenth century it was evidently quite socially acceptable to argue explicitly and openly that literacy should be treated as an exclusive club with membership reserved for the social elite. Speaking in the House of Lords in 1839 the Bishop of Exeter declared "*looking to the poor as a class, they could not expect that those who were consigned by Providence to the laborious occupations of life, should be able largely to cultivate their intellect.*"

Such a view would, of course, be inexpressible today. But in its place has developed a body of opinion that instead of arguing against mass literacy argues against the only practical means of bringing it about. This shift in position is not demonstrably a significant moral or social advance.

It is perhaps understandable that at the beginning of the twenty-first century, some people still prize their literacy as though it were membership of an exclusive club. Their easy access to reading and writing gives them a privileged advantage in life that self-interest suggests should only be shared sparingly. Their literacy makes them part of an elite and they have no interest in devaluing their membership by supporting universal admission – they want others kept out of the literacy club, just as members of, say, the Athenaeum, close ranks to exclude those who are, to adapt Margaret Thatcher's coded language, "not one of us".

Of course some of those who strive to keep the literacy club exclusive do so without being consciously aware of their bias. In fact some have convinced themselves that the outsiders have not been kept out at all, but simply remain on the outside because some innate handicap makes it inevitable that they are unfitted to climb the entrance steps. Teachers who think like that often explain children's exclusion from the 'literacy club' in this way: "*What can you expect when children have these problems?*"

For these teachers, and others like them, the idea of universal literacy is simply impossible. They believe that the world as it is – in which about one in five cannot read well – is, if not pre-ordained, certainly inevitable.

A varied range of 'problems' is used to explain why so many children make so little progress in reading. Favourite scapegoats include social and economic circumstances, home language and ethnicity, home culture and unspecified 'special needs'. These issues are sometimes referred to as 'barriers to literacy'. But the way in which these circumstances and situations are used to justify limited expectations suggests that these 'barriers' might be more accurately depicted as 'barricades', used to keep the disadvantaged safely on the outside.

No wonder anti-phonics propaganda keeps going, in the face of all the evidence and despite the innumerable times that its arguments have been shown to be false. The 'debate' is perhaps not really an argument about teaching methods at all. What seems to touch the nerve is the explicit determination to raise standards – and perhaps most controversially of all not just to raise standards for those who are safely on the road to becoming readers but also to raise standards for those who are currently left behind. To open the doors of the literacy 'club' to all.

The resistance to phonics is *in effect* just a modern-dress version of the old nineteenth-century resistance to reading. The phonics-deniers, the anxiety makers and the phonicsphobics are consciously or unconsciously heirs to those distant Jeremiahs who warned against the threat of mass literacy.

The evidence that points to this interpretation is two-fold. Firstly anti-phonics propaganda persists, despite being frequently exposed as a tissue of myths, misconceptions and falsehoods. Secondly, the alternative approach to teaching reading that the propaganda promotes in place of phonics is precisely the recipe of mixed methods and word guessing that has produced the same depressing results for around the last hundred years.

Are the anti-phonics propagandists consciously conniving at the continued exclusion from the literacy 'club' of a quarter to a fifth of people? Almost certainly not. But what matters here is not their conscious or unconscious motivation. In terms of its practical effect - its potentially disabling impact on the ambition of universal literacy - the campaign against *'phonics first, fast and only'* amounts to a sustained campaign of resistance to reading.

111

20

Resistance to Reading

A report published in 2012 estimated that 22% of the UK's population was functionally illiterate and that the cost of this to our economy was £81 billion a year, the highest such cost in Europe. The costs stem in part – but only in part – from the well-established association between low standards of education and social marginalisation. Poor reading at school is a strong predictor of social exclusion as an adult. 70% of pupils permanently excluded from school have difficulties in basic literacy skills. Adults with reading difficulties are more likely to be unemployed and more likely to be unemployed for longer periods. Low levels of literacy are also associated with poorer physical and mental health and an increased likelihood of being in trouble with the law. According to the National Literacy Trust, 25% of young offenders have reading skills below those of the average seven-year-old and 60% of the prison population has literacy difficulties.

Those with low literacy levels are at increased risk of social exclusion at the most basic level – for example, men with reading difficulties are more likely to lead solitary lives and more likely to live in households without children. Women with low levels of literacy are five times more likely to suffer from depression. Men and women with reading difficulties have lower levels of trust in others and are less likely to feel safe in their home environments.

You may search in vain for any acknowledgement of these issues in the work of the anti-phonics campaigners. They show no sign of recognition of the problem of illiteracy – let alone any compassion or any determination to put things right.

It is clear that the experience and impact of social exclusion for those on the margins is made worse when the more fortunate actively discriminate against the disadvantaged. The form of this discrimination can range from of a simple lack of sympathy to active resentment. One observer has even claimed to detect a *'demonization of the working class'*. Perhaps more robustly grounded is the view of the National Children's Bureau that British society is divided into parallel worlds in which inequality risks becoming so entrenched that "*children grow up in a state of social apartheid*". The anti-phonics campaigners are essentially siding with and actively promoting this social divide. However misguidedly, however unwittingly, however unconsciously, they have enlisted in the battalions fighting in the cause of what the National Children's Bureau calls 'social apartheid'.

In marked contrast, phonics *first, fast and only* sets out to make the process of reading accessible to all, not just those advantaged children who can figure out the code for themselves. The alphabetic principle is the key to making reading successful, meaningful and pleasurable. Children who cannot decode, or struggle to do so, are never able to become truly independent readers. And the Matthew Effect ensures that weak decoders fall further and further behind their peers.

The evidence indicates that schools commonly over-estimate children's reading ability (like the Y1 teachers who convinced themselves that children's reading was good even when they couldn't read at least 32 of the words in the Phonics Screening Check) and overlook or ignore children's reading difficulties – as, for example, reflected in the research that showed that nearly 50% of children who had entered secondary school with seriously low achievement in reading had not been included on their primary's school's register of special educational needs.

Those who are disadvantaged and at-risk include even children who have achieved National Curriculum Level 4 at the end of primary school. This level has been traditionally regarded as the benchmark for eleven-year olds but it is clear that achievement at this level includes many who have not made the progress they need to do well. Nearly half of those who achieve a lower-level 4 in English do not go on to achieve even a grade C in English at the GCSE stage. Secondary schools have repeatedly reported that the outcomes of National Curriculum English testing at the end of primary school give an unduly flattering impression of actual reading ability.

The fact that teachers consistently overestimate children's reading ability and overlook or disregard their difficulties may also at least partly explain the concern about the extent to which children read for pleasure. Children who struggle to decode are unlikely to find reading pleasurable. There is no pleasure in being bewildered by an expanse of print that cannot be turned from black marks on a page into connected meaning. Without good decoding skills, reading for pleasure is unachievable. The resistance to phonics and the dogged adherence to teaching mixed methods of word guessing is not just a barrier to reading accuracy it is significantly also a barrier to reading enjoyment.

In the nineteenth century it was possible to openly resist – even warn against - any move that threatened to spread the skills of literacy to those judged unfitted for reading and writing. But for the best part of 150 years we have had in England an educational system that on the face of it is committed to a universal entitlement to literacy. In practice this commitment has not been fulfilled. The dismal record of standards shows all too clearly that the methods used to teach reading have, for generations past, failed to extend literacy to all. Despite the advent of free compulsory education for all, the narrow determinism of the nineteenth century resisters to literacy has not been entirely thwarted.

Today, despite the abundance of scientific evidence about the critical importance of phonics, there is still resistance. This shows itself in a stubborn adherence to teaching methods that are demonstrably not successful and that are at odds with what scientific research and evidence has shown is needed. Resistance shows itself in a sustained campaign of vilification of phonics that consistently misrepresents, misleads and misinforms.

These campaigners – and the teachers who collude with them – are, ostensibly at least, in a more enlightened position that those who warned against mass literacy in the nineteenth century. Today no one echoes or consciously supports those opinions of the past. But in practice - in terms of the impact on children's reading progress and in terms of the obstacles put in the way of improvement - there seems little practical advance. Resistance to phonics *first, fast and only* is in effect a resistance to reading.

21115000R00073

Printed in Great Britain
by Amazon